RADICAL OPENNESS

Also by George Breed

Embodying Spirit: The Inner Work of the Warrior

Silence Whispers

The World's First Ever Baptist Crime Novel (Co-Author)

RADICAL OPENNESS

George Breed

iUniverse, Inc.
New York   Bloomington

Radical Openness

iUniverse books may be ordered through booksellers or by contacting:

iUniverse
1663 Liberty Drive
Bloomington, IN 47403
www.iuniverse.com
1-800-Authors (1-800-288-4677)

ISBN: 978-1-4401-3520-0 (sc)
ISBN: 978-1-4401-3521-7 (ebk)

Printed in the United States of America

iUniverse rev. date: 06/24/2009

To the One Who Breathes Me

Contents

Foreword

George Breed's latest book, *Radical Openness*, is much like the author himself: an often unexpected delight, a vitally engaging, sometimes startling pleasure, always a plangent message conveyed in an utterly unique voice. Dr. Breed has produced a work that is hard to describe in a few sentences, or even a few pages, and in this fact, one finds the book's charm as well as its impact. One comes to understand this work more through sensation than intellectual acumen because it is propelled by a peculiar apophasis, a knowing through not knowing. In fact, one may best describe this book by explaining what it is not.

Radical Openness is above all *not* a self-help book, although that, as a retired university psychologist and talented psychotherapist, is a book George certainly could have written. Nor is this, his latest offering, a manual for living a conventional spiritual life--though indeed, a robust sense of living in soul or spirit while knowing the Divine as a living reality permeates this book. For if the casual spiritual athlete were to use these writings as teachings or as guidelines constituting a spiritual path, he would quickly find himself brought to the edges of, and finally pushed beyond, all his resources and orthodox understandings to a point where the psychic determination for wholeness destroys the egoic sense of self, and one at last confronts the feasting void of Soul.

That these "irruptions of the heart" are conveyed in a lean, muscular, martial style of writing is no surprise either, for if I imagine George to be anything, I imagine him as a triple-hyphenated threat, the epitome of the warrior-philosopher-poet, and his well honed skills in the Asian martial arts are apparent in the parry, thrust, and the interwhirling play of his ideas.

Dr. Breed has often called himself a Zen Baptist, a moniker at once humorous and serious, and that honors his Protestant Georgia roots as well as the Asian psychophilospiritual tradition that has been such a profound influence in his life. It is not accurate to say he is a post-Christian or a neo-Christian, nor is he some sort of schismatic. Yet, I don't think that Zen Baptism is a sect one can easily or readily join, for in the final analysis, George is a sect of one--a Ronin--wandering but not lost, refining a singular voice and an even more singular spirit, which irrupts from the radically open-hearted nature of the Universe.

Paraphrasing Oscar Wilde, Harold Bloom wryly noted, "All bad poetry is sincere." Bad poetry conveys a too literal earnestness, a surfeit of emotion that the author plainly does not feel and, if he does, is unable to penetrate very deeply. Bad poetry is mistrustful of revealed truth--of Gnosis--and tries to hide its unartful uncertainty and inexperience by clothing itself in sincerity. Bad poetry (and bad theology, and bad thinking in general, for that matter) lacks the *salve*, the salvation, the impact, the humor, and the truthful revelation one often finds in irony. In this collection of his writing, Dr. Breed has achieved just such an ironic stance: a casually irreverent tone that exposes a powerful erudition paired with an unshakeable faith in the power of openhearted loving.

Each page of this deceptively slim volume is an embodiment of, and a benediction for radical, openhearted living in the face of an apparently profane, arbitrary, and unknowable world that constantly threatens one's survival as well as one's spirit. The beautiful revelation of this work is found in the author's willingness to face life with complete vulnerability--radical openness--which in turn reveals the sacred reality forming and informing one's familiar, material world. Living a life of radical openness establishes one firmly in the center of a sentient, responsive Universe, and by continually revolving upon and opening to our own center, the point to which we owe our own rise, the soul affords one's life a *gravitas*, a sense of presence, and wisdom.

With the publication of *Radical Openness*, Dr. George Breed obeys Walt Whitman's injunction, "That when thou must indeed come, come unfalteringly." I, for one, am very glad he did.

--Bradley Olson, Ph.D.
March 20, 2009

Preface

The hours between midnight and four a.m. are magical. In this little dark sky mountain community, no lights exist but stars, moon, my little lamp, and the green of the eyes of Kato, the temple guardian cat. Humans are snug in bed and their mental - emotional vibratory fields have vanished.

I sit quietly. Words come. I write them down.

I am not a waster of words. Maybe it comes from growing up in the hot humid South where the only relief came from an oscillating fan blowing over a block of ice and enduring the moments until the fan turned once again your way. Talk was exertion. Even having a thought would cause you to break out in a sweat. Too many thoughts could result in delirium.

As a result my writings honor brevity. Those from cooler climes write learned discourses of densely packed words in sentences so long you forget what the subject was when you finally reach the object.

To my chagrin, my writings look suspiciously like poetry. I resonate with that wild man Rumi who wrote: *"By God, I detest poetry. In my eyes there is nothing worse…"*

But what are you going to do with terse irruptions from the heart?

Acknowledgments

Deep appreciation to Cathy Gazda, soul friend, and cover designer for this book and the other three I authored or co-authored. I chuckle at the little red airplane and, Lord knows, a chuckle these days is worth ten zillion billion million of those electronic blips we trade for food.

Love and admiration to my partner, Karen Mattingly. My hike-master, she leads me into places of impossible beauty and leaves me standing gasping (yes, I mean it both ways). The masterful photo Karen took that is the back cover proves the point. No matter how many fantastic places we hike into, she tells me there is one more that will just knock my socks off! I keep believing her and, thus far, she has proven absolutely right. Thank you, Karen.

Psychologist, ex - street cop, myth-o-metician, lover of Shakespeare and Rilke and Jung and Nietzsche (I could go on), quoter of the exactly correct poem and literary passage at the exactly correct moment, drinker of coffee while engaging in wild (untamed) and no-bounds conversation, author of the Foreword, Brad Olson is a friend's friend and for that I thank you!

And of course, a bow to Kato the Samurai Cat, who meditates quietly in his favorite catatonic poses during these writing hours.

Come Dance the Mutanto

God Chant

When Silence stirred Itself and opened to the creation of the universe, Silence made three sounds.

The first sound is AHHHHH! Room is created.
The second sound is OOOOOOO! Infinite possibility is born.
The third sound follows naturally—MMMMMMMMMM!
The taste of appreciation is now here.

We express these sounds.
We allow these sounds to come through us.

We are co-creators with the Great Mystery.
We make these sounds as we open to creation.

AHHHHH! Room to create is born.
OOOOOOO! The sound of wonder at the infinite possibilities that lie before us.
MMMMMMMM! The sound of appreciation as the creative work/play begins
and we "taste" what is unfolding.

We sing/chant a song to God.

AH-AH-EY-YEH!
O-O-EY-YEH!
MM-MM-EY-YEH!

And David Danced Before The Lord With All His Might

Doggone it! Just like Bre'r Rabbit, I keep getting stuck (sticking myself) in the tar baby of lower existence. I know better but it's such an easy target, sitting there all smug and dumb. See! There I go again! Looking at the tar baby instead of the path.

Instead of hopping down the honey trail,
I decide to engage in a round of fisticuffs with the stuporous.
Haven't I learned by now? The stupor I see is the stupor of me.

My beloved teacher Hey-Sous
(who just looks at me sometimes and shakes his head)
says to let the dead bury the dead.

"But what about the condition of the world?" I ask.

"This is not a weeding party, Jaw-Edge (he has a southern accent)," he sez. "It's a wedding party! You need to come on over, kiss the bride and groom, and dance with their mama and daddy!"

Let's see. Hmmmmm….

Instead of standing around staring at this corpse, p'd off because it's doing the natural corpse thing with rottenness and decay, I am to join the wedding party.

Tough choice! Part of me likes kicking corpses and tar babies around and being all upset about the human condition.

I look from one to the other.
Corpse. Wedding. Wedding. Corpse.

Wedding!

I find my rapt presence.

I hear the music as I approach the open door….

I joy in the celebration.

Come Dance The Mutanto!

FLASH! BREAKING NEWS! THIS JUST IN!
The Anthropods are out and the Mutantos are in.

All this can be explained and described
in a nice orderly scholarly way,
but you would not read it.

You have been living in Anthropod-land too long.
Your brain is set to respond to quick news flashes,
to commercial bursts of sound and color.

Attention deficit disorder is no longer a disorder,
it is the common consciousness.

So FLASH! An evolutionary jump has happened!
A leap to a new species!
No matter what the anthropod press and the anthropod tv
and the anthropod magazines say, the anthropods are old news.

The anthropods have had their chance and screwed it all to hell.
To their credit, they looked to take care of their own
but the definition of "their own" was too small.

You remember the anthropods don't you?
The ones who just about killed it all off?

The ones who fought desperately to put a world back together
that wasn't apart in the first place?
Dead end blind alleys of evolution turning around and around
in their fashionable cul-de-sacs so fast they were kissing their own butts,
noses firmly up their own asses,
thinking that sweet smell was the nectar of nirvana?

BREAKING NEWS!
The universe is diverting its energies,
its creative flow in other directions.
Anthropods are old news now, staggering toward extinction.

The universe, forever creative,
is even now giving birth to the Mutantos,
the next round in the spiraling of the universe embodying.

The anthropods were Mutantos once until they went insane,
splitting their minds from their bodies, making merchants king,
ruthlessly eradicating whatever got in their way.

A small test. If you are going HUNH?
you are probably in your anthropod mode.
If some part of you is going YES! that part is Mutanto.

Cultivate your Mutanto, my friend.
Lay up your treasures in Mutanto-land.
Burst out of your anthropod and dance the Mutanto!

LIVE HAPPENING NEWS!
Anthropods are out and Mutantos are in!

On The Trail

Hiking a trail this morn, I met a woman staggering around,
a cell phone swallowing her head.
I thought of calling 911,
but I had no phone and hers was busy.

Family Reunion

The arrow positions itself on my heart and clicks twice.
My mind screen disappears. Everything refreshes, reloads.

My eyes open in awe.

Jesus is no longer a victim.
He sits here as big brother.

Buddha no inscrutable eastern potentate.
He and Jesus look in each other's eyes and laugh.

Moses, Solomon, and David joke and skip rocks across the river.
Muhammad plays marbles with the kids.

Brahma, Vishnu, and Siva toss the salad,
creating, sustaining, releasing into the ever new.

Lao Tzu, that yamabushi, teaches us Zing Tao.

Wakantanka's drum laughs and sings.

The picnic is on!

My hard drive has dissolved
into the software of our Source.

Cow Check

Checking out my sacred cows for hoof and mouth disease,
finding all I **hold** as holy is rotten to the core.

All the quicksilver cows are still with me.
The rest are roaming free.

I do not grasp all I truly love.

Direct Connection

If we could Google a map of the world's spiritual state,
as per the human contribution, the map would
fluctuate with each shift in my and your consciousness.

Capacity

When I lean and when I cling,
I get in trouble.

A lean is the beginning of a fall.
A cling is the grasping of a straw.

An avalanche will soon occur.
A drowning is about to happen.

This aching place, this hole
won't be filled with a lean,
won't be assuaged with a cling.

This discomfort must be opened wider.

No leaning. No clinging.
I am developing my capacity.

Bibliophile

We are the writings in this book of life.
We are the soundings of each page.

Blank until our blood, the ink,
flows through the bumps and surges
of the pulsing of our lives.

Whole chapters written
pressed between the pages
like flowers of long ago

hieroglyphs of a time gone by
pictographs of fading meaning

Shaking clear
letting go
leaping free falling splashing
across this page
and pages yet to come.

Transfiguration

The Eternal Sinner

"I am not come to call the righteous, but sinners to repentance"
(Matthew 9:13)

In this case, I would rather be a sinner than righteous. When righteous, we have very little capacity for change, feeling we have the entire universe contained within our teacup. A sinner is one who has great capacity, who quaffs huge drafts of the unknown every day. Jesus loves the sinners, spurns the righteous. " Let the dead bury the dead," he says. You can't do anything with the righteous but the sinners are prime ground for great transfiguration. I pray we may be eternal sinners eternally transforming always walking into and through the open door.

Intersection

The cross. The horizontal arm of linear time with our pasts and our futures and the making something of ourselves. The vertical post, grounded in the earth while opening to the divine, to that which calls us into being every moment. We live at the intersection.

From "above" within, the dove eternally dives and we are the cosmos embodying. From "within" without, the radiance of the heart is the embodying cosmosing. The dove dive and the heart radiance are simultaneous wonderments.

White With Foam

you slather a thin veneer
of fantasy over reality
then live within that slather

the heart is much more huge

when you flip it
so that the ocean is above
and foam below
you are a bottom feeder
living on the crumbs of the divine

in this sense
living in the depths
is superficial

when awareness
opens to the ocean
you will cry
o my god

Love Sounds

Before the beginning,
There was No Thing.

The Source breathed out....
Three Sounds

A-A-A-A-A-A
Ahhhh!

Room appeared
Room for All

O-O-O-O-O-O
Ohhhh!

Infinite possibility opened
Birds, cyclones, quarks,
land mass, elves, giraffe,
genii, aurora boreal, hump-backed whales
All possible

M-M-M-M-M-M
Yummmm!

Chocolate was born
Baby dumplings
Sweet grass
Everything an éclair filled with Love
And It Was Good

Our Source, the Origin, keeps singing, is singing now!
A-A-A-A-A-A-O-O-O-O-O-O-M-M-M-M-M-M

Making Room for All,
Infinite Uniqueness,
Creations of Love

And so we cannot help but sing…

Ah Yes!
O Baby!
Mmmmmmm….

OM again!

The Deliciousness of Night

Long have I roamed awake while others slept.

This deliciousness of night when things change shape.
Rocks move.
Stars cruise.
Moon laughs.
Trees whisper to each other of what they have seen.
Earth creaks as it spins.

Cat snoozes in the ecstatic sphinx position.

And this one, with the night, taking joy in
this embodying, this human trance-mutation.

Trance Ended

A light around one's head

does not mean one is holy,

but that one has transcended

rational consciousness

and opened to

integral consciousness.

Formerly, we stuck such folk

in a worship box.

Now, we are becoming them.

Out Of Darkness

I sit disconsolate, forlorn.

God Himself overshadows me with His wings,
wipes the tears from my eyes,
touches my forehead with the tip of His finger.

Sit up, He says.

I sit like Buddha all ablaze,
Jesus praying within my heart.

Stand up, He says.

I come to Life.

Let's go, He says.

We walk,
old friends,
holding hands.

Transfiguration

I wish to call this to your attention:
your animal is dying.

It's like Yeats said, we are
"fastened to a dying animal."

We arrange its floral hair,
buttress and bolster its sag,
drape its decay with new material

and I admire these valiant efforts
but I wish to call this to our attention:
our animal is dying.

I know you know
and may not wish to face this.
It is not talked of amongst the polite.

I say it anyway. Our animal is dying.

And while I'm on the topic I must report:
our noumenal is thriving.

Our essence, our high spirit,
angel at the ladder's very top,
our noumenal is thriving.

Animal matter, dense spirit, is on the wane.

Noumenal spirit, the lightest matter, is unfolding.

Our animal is dying.

Our noumenal is thriving.

What wonderment!

This breathing as this earth!

All Birds Uncaged

I soar with the Wind,
all birds uncaged

I sing to the Unborn
the Living much too busy
sunk in dense matter
forever suffering

always making something of it
or wishing to but can't

I feel like a Ghost at my own funeral
saying it's all fine but they can't hear

except for those making toasts
taking turns leaping over the corpse

Ah well,
I blend with the Wind
the Unborn join in the singing

All birds uncaged

Spiritual Intelligence

With spiritual awareness
we recognize

each of us
is a center of the universe;

we have no bounds;
the "inner" infinity and the "outer" infinity are the same infinity;
we are the gateless gate between the "inner" and the "outer";
eternity is now;

we are constantly changing while going nowhere;
we are constantly dying and being reborn;
the ego is a self-created vehicle
for the fulfillment of desire and a sense of security;

universal energies and wisdom pour through us
as we surrender and open;

spiritual intuition allows more powerful understanding
than do reason and emotion;

we are co-creators with our Source,
who is like a circle with no circumference
whose center is everywhere;

relentless compassion is a key transformational energy;

all things, including individuals, are inter-relational
and have no substance on their own;

we are energetic beings,
subsets of a vast Realm of Energy
we can only begin to imagine;

our every thought, feeling, and action
reverberates throughout the entire universe.

Luv

So after I knew luv in my heart,
I went and got all these here books
over my lifetime and read them to see
what others were seeing and saying life is all about
so I would not be fooled into some little box
of my own making and what it all came down to
was luv -- a radiance of being extending to infinity
in all directions, unimpeded -- which is what
I knew all along, and that's okay for now I know
more luv language and my mind is more expansive
and inclusive which is a sure sign of luv and I feel happy
that what I know interwhirls with such good fit
with these thinkers and writers across centuries and cultures
and paths and occupations so that we have become
like a tiger chasing itself around the tree until it became butter
to be served on good hot pancakes and ain't that luv?

Engaging

Release the clutch.

Weeping & Rejoicing

Jesus Wept

sometimes i think if i were the creator i would just hit the cosmic reset button -- take it all back to zero -- start again -- just the earth part i reckon -- the rest seems to be doing okay -- the humans seem like such a botched-up group -- everyone hating everyone -- seeing themselves as the chosen ones -- the others as ratfink lizards low on the evolutionary scale -- apologists for each grouping on blogs, in books, and churches using creative wit sardonic humor bombastic putdowns -- amassing pep rally clusters of the righteous -- calling on god to kill the godless -- group a killing group b and group b killing group a because it's the right thing to do -- and as always men, women, children, mothers, fathers, sisters, brothers, uncles, grandmothers, aunts, grandfathers blown to smithereens -- body parts everywhere -- the way we always do it -- the way we have always been -- murderous righteous two-leggeds still using the kindergarten argument: it's all their fault

Bodhisattva Irony

I have taken a vow
not to enter heaven
until all others have entered.

So will you please
get with the program?

The Value Of A Room Is Its Room

Many of us cannot bear the thought,
much less the practice, of emptiness.

"O No! I must be full of thoughts and plans
and worries and anxieties and schemes."

"I cannot bear any silence. I know I'll disappear."

"Keep the television or radio or ipod cranking.
Let me make calls on my cell phone."

"O please! Do not let me face myself.
I know that I'm not there. Or if I am,
I'm way too horrible or boring to be with."

Our unwillingness to simply be
throws us in our cars,
propels us to the malls,
to an endless succession of dealers
where we look to satisfy our junkie habits
and fill ourselves with the sweet relief of purchase.

Or we dive into our chosen fix,
whatever it may be, our work, our sex,
our abstruse philosophical thought, our politics, our sports.

We make ourselves an occupied territory,
bombarding ourselves with sound and light and fury.

The closest we come to emptiness is stupor.

"No! No! No! No Emptiness!"

"I'm going to keep myself distracted until I die!"

A-pneuma-gnosis

The fear of being spiritually whole;
the fear of seeing God face-to-face;
the fear of opening to direct perception of Reality;
the fear of Real-Eye-Zing;
and the ensuing retreat into the disease of *phenomenonitis.*

The Suffering of God

God is being born,
and we are the raw material.
Heaven help him.

An I Doll Is An Eye Dull

Each of us has an i.

We love our i and wish to preserve it. We like the thought of our i living forever.

The i suffers and by suffering proves itself alive. Why does i suffer? Because i is a defense against life itself.

Like an irritant in an oyster, i refuses to become the oyster. Instead i becomes a pretty little bauble, treasured by other i's. i wants to be in the i hall of fame.

In written English, i is a capital offense, standing alone in priapic splendor – **I**

We like the i-deal of transcending our i. As i works to transcend the i, i gets stronger. i thinks the i-glow from this spiritual workout is a sign of an enlightened being.

i gives up.

And then i starts practicing giving up as a means to i's salvation.

i is so funny.

i is an i-con.

Drift

Mind drifting drifting
like gently blown snow
across vast plains

finally piling
up against

some old fence post
of a memory
erected long ago
still standing

heartwood split by nails
ringed with barbed wire

cold
drifting
snow

piling up

surrounding
soothing
this old wound

Relationship Game # 413

as long as i sit in my shit,
i will sit in my shit

you are to blame
for me sitting in my shit

you left
so i shit myself

it always happens this way
people leave me and i shit myself

i will sit in my shit
as long as i sit in my shit

i look for love from others
and can't find it so i shit myself

i am not shitting you
this is the way i do it

i shit you not
i shit myself

The Roller Coaster of Doom

It has always been the case that the existing universe takes "the world"

into a screaming dive of what looks like extinction and certain doom

and zoooom! pulls out and up into new realms of transformation.

This is happening right now.

Quit cowering and fussing.

Enjoy the ride!

Dream

Covered my face,
closed my eyes,
and cried

for mistakes, missteps, illusions

I wept, aching
from some deep place
shuddering upward into tears

heart tearing like split silk

HermesAphrodite

i am tuned to the sadness in women
and to the rowdiness in men

they have both been used
as weapons against me

so i in turn
learned them well

i know despair so deep
the bottom falls out

and exuberance so expansive
i've been thrown out of bars

they both lead to one place
these two energetic streams

laughter

deep and open
laughter

Eye Kisses

...some words are so beautiful,
some sentences so enchanting,
the eyes wish to caress them forever....

Ever Body Thinx

ever body thinx they are the star of the universe
the whole thing leaping into being for one sole purpose
the creation of them
and frustrated and wondering
why ever body else doesn't get this
and fall in line

Down Dark Deep

what do you think that is?

that place aching inside
aching and yearning

that itchiness

o for heaven's sake don't scratch it

must you always seek conclusion?
flatlining into the same old zombie?

what do you think that is?
that voice calling?

deep dark down

Lord Lord

i know that dreamscape land of baptist fervor allowing men of god to don klan robes leading haters in prayer in the glare of a gargantuan burning cross can't drink a beer but you can get intoxicated on hate praise the lord as long as you keep that thin veneer of sanctification praise god and sex is not to be mentioned but is alright undercover in the dark with the woman in the inferior position the way god meant her to be and wait till your father comes home and dad beating on naked butts with his belt in all righteousness and the full approval of mom and god and always always you are to do god's will which the preacher knows for sure and is not hesitant to tell you in his cocky brashness and in the name of jesus who everybody knows came to earth to be a champion for america against all them heathen out there lord lord no wonder i became a psychologist

Tragicomedy

I want something.

I light up God like a match and go looking around.

When I find it, I blow him out and throw him away.

It's just part of the human comedy.

The light by which we look is the light we seek.

Warrior

Intranaut

A meta-construct came in the early a.m., *Intranaut*.

"Naut" is a Greek term for sailor. There are *astro*nauts and *cosmo*nauts, even *aero*nauts – those who sail the skies and cosmos, those who voyage the outer infinity.

Intra means, of course, inner or within. An intranaut is one who sails the seas of inner infinity. An intranaut is a voyager into the mysteries of the inner realms.

An intranaut is a warrior, a mystic, a healer, a shaman, mindfully aware, and as such, highly intuitive. Without these qualities, there would not be the courage to leap into inner space.

Zing Tao

Life doesn't seem all that complicated.
It all boils down to a few categories.

1. Entertaining the monkey
2. Walking through the structure
3. Engagement and quick action
4. Reflection and second thought
5. Never mind

Gnosis

I think I know in which closets
the skeletons genuflect
and where the gold is buried.
I think I know what is wrong
with your mother.
I think I know what God has for lunch
and whom he uses for a serviette.
Though this day is gray, my mood is good.

Sedona Hike

Water dissolves rock,
the hardest rock.
Be like water.

Air evaporates water,
the widest water.
Be like air.

The insubstantial
has its way with
the substantial.

Counting Coup On God

Riding into the mystery
I touch the "Other,"
Powers merging.

God counters,
galloping into my secret hidden camp,
staring into my surprised eyes with loving glee.

Spirit Forging

The forging of spirit
consists of training so hard
we forget who we are

dropping those tired old stories
of Me and Who I Am

those melodramas we use
to fritter away our lives

(hello, my name is _____
and i'm a fritteraholic)

The forging of spirit
is training so deeply
all interest is lost in pulling
this self together (re-member-ing)
in the same old,
tired old, old, old ways.

No more rouge on that corpse face.

Throw me in the fire!
Heat me white hot!
Shape me anew!

The Altar Of The Holy

There are reasons the shaman
lives on the distant perimeter
of the village.

Exile can make one bitter
or open one to unlimited vision.

This knife is honed,
scraped back and forth
on the rough edges of society
for many years.

I place it on the altar of the Holy
as an instrument of healing.

Not my will, but Thine be done.

Amen.

Meeting the Necessary in the Wilderness

And he was there in the wilderness forty days, tempted of Satan; and was with the wild beasts; and the angels ministered unto him. Mark 1:13

Jesus went into the wilderness to meet his Necessary. (Do I have to explain why Satan is Jesus' Necessary? I think not.) As thesis and antithesis, they arose from and are contained within the same Ground. Like a pair of scissor blades they kept each other sharp.

In the wilderness encounter they cut against each other. The Necessary making anticuts, bringing a whole cloth of spun and woven imaginings into existence with each snick. Jesus countering, making clean sharp slices through these tempting veilings.

Jesus went into the wilderness a scissor,
one blade of a cutting pair, and came out a sword.

Maybe After I'm Dead

Now I don't want to hear all that stuff about relaxing in the now and mindfulness is the cure to it all and lotus-sit into the Ohm. Don't try to calm me down. I'm on an adventure, dammit! I'm having conversations with God.

Warrior of Spirit

I have no home. The universe is my home.

I have no clothes. I stand naked in the universe.

I have no sword. Spirit is my sword.

I have no horse. This breath is my horse.

I have no dog. My mind is my dog.

I have no map. Infinity is my map.

I have no heart. Life's rhythm is my heart.

I have no mind. Vast openness is my mind.

I have no security. The unknown is my security.

I have no intelligence. Awareness is my intelligence.

I have no enemies. Attachment is my enemy.

I have no ruler. The ruler of rulers is my ruler.

I have no place to go. Here now is my place to go.

I have no family. All sentient beings are my family.

I have no apology. Lovingkindness is my apology.

I have no sorrow. Laughter is my sorrow.

I have no gratitude. Joy is my gratitude.

WWJACHD

My two favorite Warriors of Spirit are Jesus and Crazy Horse.

They have much in common.

Each dared all and risked everything.

Each gave little or no thought to his own safety.

They counted themselves as dead already and were able to fully live.

Jesus and Crazy Horse owned very little "stuff."

Their hearts and souls and bodies and spirits
were dedicated to the Lifeforce that breathes us.

Jesus and Crazy Horse gave their all.

They cared for the poor and hungry and despised.

They put themselves last.

Jesus and Crazy Horse hated evil and lived the truth.

They walked right into the camps of the insane devourers of life and counted coup.

They never gave up.

Jesus and Crazy Horse refused to be governed. No one could do a thing with them.

They were in tune with nature.

They could sleep on the ground and build a one-match fire.

The very existence of Jesus and Crazy Horse proclaimed
enduring resistance to split-minded shrivelization.

Jesus and Crazy Horse are brothers.

Jesus and Crazy Horse are true Warriors of Spirit, role models for us all.

Clothes

Church

I worship at the Church of Our Lady of Perpetual Transformation.
I never know what to wear or what to bring.
So I go naked.

The Shape I'm In

Let me keep climbing out of every structure ever made

Not resting in the corpse of days gone by

Let formlessness be my form

No container ever fully holding

Wearing No Close

everyone of us has a mindset
which both defines us and confines us

we struggle to extricate ourselves
from that which was once our salvation
our protection against the onslaught and holy terror of being

the armor has become a tomb
we look to wear silk instead of steel
or better yet go naked
like a laughing squealing child run free.

Kool Whip On Bed Rock

Ah bin thin king whut doo ah no aftur ahl theez yeers?

Whin yew skrape uhway whut ah bin tawwt iz troo
buy sewsigheetea ann cherch, skrape dahn tew bed rok,
whin yew git rat dahn tew it,
ah no nut thin

utha then sum thin iz breethin mee
mekkin mee uhlive

yeh uh yeh uh
ah no ahl thee fillosofuhkuhl theereez
thee metuhfizzuhkuhl vewz
thee theeohlodgeuhkuhl stuhff

butt thay r jus ohverrlaaz
kool whip on thee bed rok

ah pey know mind
ah luv mah frennz
ah luv liv in
ah luv skie ann urth

ah luv whut breethz mee

bed rock uh bye behbeh

Let's See! The Swim Suit Or The Tux?

Holy Clothes and Sacred Ambulations!!!

What kind of clothes do we have to wear to talk with God?
What posture and what stance? What tone of voice?
Must one be a chanting gymnast?

Does God say Hey now! I like that outfit!
Do that fitness yoga pose you showed me the other day!

A posture can become an imposition.
Look out! We may find ourselves praying to our prayer!

Rather than donning clothes, Moses kicked off his shoes.
Jonah wore a whale. Enoch walked around.
Ruth worked in the fields. Mary sang exuberantly.
Jesus climbed a mountain. Dogen cooked the food.
Dorothy Day fed the hungry.
Thich Nhat Hanh washed the dishes.

The clothing and the posing are for us.
They help us get bare naked.

And a bare naked heart is always heard by its Lover.

Terminally Naked

It's best some planes take off without you

loaded with the luggage of your logo,
that contrived design you flash around.

Don't go looking for your baggage
Let it fly. Wave bye-bye!

Cruise in your rent-a-car
content and chuckling
into the new unknown.

The first part of our lives
we keep adding layers of clothes.
We are this and we are that.

The later part of our lives
we shed it all, naked and delicious.

Best ship that luggage now.

To leave here wearing clothes is unbecoming.

Locked In

And what do you see all day but your own eyes looking?

What do you hear all day but your own alarm?

What do you touch but your own sensation?

What is the odor you smell but your own nose?

Wrapped up in yourself like that how can you help but chase your own tale?

Come on out of there, you little rascal!

Evaporate the walls of your mind!

Following My Cauling

I've got to get this caul off my head
and I find it hard to shake.

Have tried scraping it against raw jagged zen bones
with some relief. The itching goes away.

A good wine or a long walk
also seems to work pretty well.

I sing within my caul. It's still here
but I don't mind so much.

The caul keeps me from seeing clearly.
I sit within it at a never-ending end of a hall of mirrors.
All I can see is my own reflection.
All I can see is what I can see.

I've got to get this caul off my head or I will go insane.
Maybe I already am.

I entertain myself by saying
well at least I don't have my head stuck up my ass.

I have been told that if I join certain clubs my caul will go away.
That would be like trading one caul for another.
Or even worse, I'd be double-bagged.

Sometimes I insert my head into the tv,
the land of talking caulheads who tell me what is going on.
I don't believe them though. I know they only see their cauls.

Like a cell of hooded terrorists, they affirm to each other
that the stance they are taking is absolutely correct
and that the hood they are wearing is not a hood at all
but absolute reality.

I click off the tv and sit quietly within my own cauling.
The cat looks at me with his cat caul.

I arise and go to work on my upcoming seminar:
Not to Worry: It's Just A Head Caul.

The Art And Fun Of Relentless Openness

Received an email from a friend asking
if there is an exercise
that can assist the practice of relentless opening.
Here is the reply that emerged.

Yessir, relentless lovingkindness and relentless openness go together.

As for an exercise, whatever you are thinking limits openness.
Whatever images you are entertaining set their own boundaries.
When we are thinking and/or imaging, we are living in second-order reality,
a realm one-step removed from the universe unfolding.

The exercise is to become aware of the bubblehead world.
Simply acknowledge "I am now in the bubble head world"
when you are in the bubble head world. This is a huge step.

Watch the bubblehead images as they move through.
Now they are this way. Now that way. Now they are of her.
Now they are of him. Now they are of us. Now they are of me.
Now they are what iffing. Now they are....

Now I am thinking about my watching the images.
Now I am wondering if it is having any effect.
Now I am watching my thinking and the imagery of my thinking.
Now I am thinking that my thinking will never subside.
Now I am thinking that my thinking that my thinking will never subside is funny.
Now I am thinking that my thinking that it's funny that my thinking
that my thinking will never subside is hilarious.
Now I am laughing.
Now....

Do this relentlessly. It provides an opening.

Now I am thinking that I am hoping that this helps.

Now I laugh about thinking that I'm hoping....
George

Clothes

I'm summoned to potential jury duty this morning
and I don't have a thing to wear! What? You mean this old rag?

Luckily (and deliberately) I live in Flagstaff where attire is not the issue.
Folk pretty much dress however they want.

We've all seen (or perhaps worn) the flip-flops / shorts / down jacket
ensemble.
Then there's the long-skirted earth muffin look.
River runners, cowboys and girls, bikers (motorized and not),
Navaho, Hopi, Apache, aging and youthful hippies,
and idiosyncratic Colorado Plateau dwellers of all types
produce an ever-fascinating fashion parade.

I remember some city dwellers coming to Flagstaff
and looking to enforce a dress code on those they thought they ruled.
They just couldn't quite get it that heels and panty hose
don't cut it on a snowy icy mountain community day.

I like what Jesus had to say about clothes. His students asked him:
When will you appear to us and when shall we see you?

He answered: *When you strip off your clothes without being ashamed,*
and you take your clothes and put them under your feet
like little children and trample them,
then you will see the son of the living one and you will not be afraid.

That Jesus! So unshrivelized!

If I go to jury selection naked this morning,
I don't think they will listen to my reason
— that I want to see Jesus.

But I think I'll go as naked as I can beneath my clothes.

Zen Baptist

Zen Baptist

Some twenty years ago, I was riding shotgun with a man across the cactused desert of southern Arizona. Being a religious man of the Protestant variety, he asked me what my faith was. When I said Zen Baptist, he actually shuddered in horror. I thought he was going to drive off the road. "Don't say that again," he said. "Don't ever say that again."

Well, here I am saying it again.

I don't understand the horror of it.

The word *Zen* is a Japanese derivation of the Chinese *cha'n* which is derived from the Sanskrit *dhyana* which means "meditation."

Meditation as I understand and practice it is not just sitting meditation. It means being in a meditative state **all the time**. Meditation is no zoned-out state. It is clear crisp open awareness. I first learned this Zen way from the martial arts and know its strong and sound value.

Baptist refers to a bunch of people who love and follow Jesus and his teachings. Well, I do. I don't go along with a lot of the Baptist doctrine, which I tend to see as dogma, but the Baptists are my roots, and like The Dalai Lama says, you are to respect your roots. They remain your roots no matter what you do.

So. No way around it. I'm a Zen Baptist.

Here are a few zen baptist poesy's.

Soan So

I come from the lineage of Soan So, a Zen teacher of great renown unknown by anyone. Soan So had an interesting style of teaching. Here are some of his sayings.

Soan So said: "Other teachers give you problems to be solved (koans). I give you solutions to be made a problem of (soans)."

Soan So said: "Do you want solve-ation?
First you have to create a problem."

Soan So said: "We are in training to be who we already are.
We are wholly fools."

Soan So said: "Nothing mattering forms the universe."

Soan So said: "Nothing can fill the whole within you."

Soan So said: "No person can fill the hole of your yearning."

Soan So said: "Surrender! You Bozo!"

Soan So said: "Give It Up!"

Soan So said: "You knot head! Full of what-knots! And why-knots!"

Soan So said: "If you are knot-going, then by all means, think how-knot!"

Sometimes we would knot off during knotting practice.
Soan So would shout: "Do knot!"

In the midst of an evening of sake hilarity after extensive knotting practice, Soan So said: "O what tangled skeins we weave in our efforts to believe!"

Breathing

Our breathing has a natural rhythm.
Inbreathing, pause, outbreathing, pause.

In our spiritual breath,
the pause is where God lives.

Breathing in, we breathe in grace and mercy.
Breathing out, we breathe out lovingkindness.

Pausing, we sit with God.

Round and Round

Ladies and gentlemen! In this corner we have Nothing!
(Applause and cheers and boos)
And in the opposite corner we have Everything!
(Cheers and boos and stamping of feet)

We will have two rounds
which will occur simultaneously!

In the Round of the Absolute,
Nothing is mattering while Everything matters.

In the Round of the Relative,
Everything is mattering while Nothing matters.

Get ready! Get set!

Go!

New Jesus Shoes

Wear your new Jesus shoes all you want
but don't try to stuff me in your shoe box.

My situation is different from yours.

I need to get more lost, not more found!

Mister Zen & Mister Baptist

Being zenbaptist is creatively amusing.

The zen part knows that words obscure
and lives in silent vibrancy
with swift immediate action.

The baptist part wallpapers
the universe with words,
wants to explain it all
in a story so profound
that folk can't help but
jump up and be saved.

Mister zen sometimes sits on mister baptist
as if he is a meditation cushion.

Mister baptist throws mister zen
toothy chunks of verbiage, meaty thought,
to see how he will respond.

An odd couple:
mister zero and mister one.
If you don't know which is which,
mister baptist will explain.

Zero Tolerance

"God has chosen the foolish things of the world to confound the wise"
--I Corinthians 1:27

When you think you know something, you don't know nothing.
All you got is a swelled head. And some turf to defend that nobody
really cares about, except some other head swellers.

And that includes creeds, statements of faith, and manifestos.

It's a new world, boys and girls. No clinging!

Time to be a holy fool, wholly a fool.

As I must continue to repeat, God is a circle with no circumference whose
center is everywhere. As my friend Joan reminded me this morning, God's
numerical sign is zero, O.

That is also the sign of a fool.

Dissolve me into zero, O God!
Let your foolishness and my foolishness be the same.
I wish to flunk all my tests of competence and become a Zero!

Security Is Total Abandon

No need to spin the fabric
and don the clothing of a secondary reality.
Stand naked in this universe

No need to "put a head
on top of your head."
Shake free of all ill-ooze-ion

Where is that joy
you so casually tossed aside
like a spent undergarment?

Here now! Real yourself in!

Hey now! Let yourself go!

Hey Here! Open that beautiful heart of yours!

The whole universe dances and sings!

One Begins With O

the 0 and the 1
the womb and the phallus

the cup and coffee spoon
empty tomb and cross

wide open receptivity, defiant uprightness
"her love is boundless" and "he's such a standup guy"

polytheism, monotheism
the wyrd of interweaving, the penetration of history

all of us and the I that is me
inclusive and exclusive

the circle with no circumference whose center is everywhere
and the one and only god you must serve or rot in hell

zen and baptist
no-self and person of distinction

zero one

Which Does The Dunking:
The Basketball Or The Hoop?

While B and I were sitting yakking in the early morning sun outside the downtown coffee shop, he suddenly wondered aloud what a zen baptism is or would be like. We didn't give it much time because we were on to other things, but I believe we quickly agreed it would entail total immersion with no clinging.

A little experiential reflection on this grave and resurrective matter gives imagery of the dunker, the dunked, and the dunking substance as the same water. The infinity "outside" and the infinity "inside" are the same infinity.

In linear time, the immersion and uprising, the burial of the old and forthcoming of the new, are occurring every nanosecond. Compared to a nanosecond ago, Behold! I am a new creature!

In no-time, baptism is occurring spontaneously. The old is dying and the new a'borning simultaneously. Not even a razor's edge of distance between. Not even a between.

Crossover

The great chasm widens.
We are over here now.
Crucifixion victimology fading away.

We have stepped over.
Don't cross Jesus.
He's dancing round.

The Final Word

I know that from a certain point of view I am not supposed to find this amusing, but I do. And I think that God probably gets a chuckle out of it too.

In the book of Revelation which has been placed at the end of the Christian Holy Book, the author writes (at the end of the last chapter) that no one better add anything to this book (some think he is referring to the entire Bible) or all the plagues will come down on them. He then proceeds to add four more sentences and two Amens!

That sets me to chuckling. Chuckling and smiling at the foibles of us humans (that "us" includes me). We can get so serious! And when we get too serious, we make donkeys of ourselves.

"And this book is about God's love, and if you mess with it, you are going to suffer and suffer BAD!"

That doesn't sound like God to me. It sounds like a human all worked up into some kind of righteous frenzy. But rather than my getting all worked up about his getting all worked up, I just laugh.

And then, in the Bible I am looking at right now (the 1599 Geneva Bible), as if to drive the point home, somebody added the capitalized words "THE END".

After that, someone went even further, in the 1611 King James version of the Bible, and put a period afterward: "THE END." I wonder what will be next, an exclamation mark? THE END!

Maybe you don't have the same sense of humor I do. Mine comes, as a psychologist, from listening to humans over the years trying to convince themselves and other humans that their version of the truth is really THE truth and the others better get in line. Period.

Sometimes I laugh. Sometimes I just shake my head.

The Unordained

i continue to find boring
all religious metaphoring
god is this and god is that
with the answers all down pat
i love the open gaze of zen
with all existing as my kin

Bye Bye

i done said it ever way i know
guess i got a one-cell brain
so here it is and i'm outta here, i'm gone

one more time—

if you want to chop it up
and make one part top dog
and the other under
just go right ahead

i got no desire to do so
wanna know my church?
well i'll tell you anyway
IS
the everlovin' church of IS

A Great Open Heart

When I was a boy, a great-aunt gave me a silver cross
with a small silver man nailed to it. I did not know what to do with it.
I knew she thought it was of great value.
After a few days, I dug a deep hole in the back yard and buried it.
In later life, I realized that my boyish instincts were true and real.

I love Jesus. I do not love what we have made of him.

Some say that Jesus was a blood sacrifice to appease his father
who will hold a grudge against us forever if we do not come to the cross
and bathe in his son's blood. It's a gruesome domestic violence story.

We humans killed him and we say God did it
— that it was God's plan for us to kill him.

This torture of a free spirit is an example of the dark side of tribalism.
You are not one of us, not in our group, so we are going to nail you.
It still occurs. Frequently.

Though many take this emphasis
upon the nailing and the cross for granted now,
to revere an instrument of torture is most peculiar.

Two thousand years of generations of humans
have been born into this way of thinking.

One way to jar yourself out of it is to answer the question –
what if Jesus had been born into a time
when political offenders and shakers
of the establishment were electrocuted?

Atop every church would be an electric chair,
folk would wear little electric chairs
on chains around their necks and dangling from their ears.

The pious would enter churches
and make the sign of the electric chair,
would worship at the stations of the chair.

The symbol of Jesus is not an instrument of torture,

The symbol of Jesus is a great open heart.

Transubstantiation

I do not worship
the little normal god

the marvel of fitness and health
working out in his cosmic gym

the one with manners
who serves as Dear Abby for us all

I worship the raw naked God
of many heads and eyes

unafraid of assuming paradoxical shape

devouring self with massive jaws
and springing forth anew

I love the voracious God
consuming us with fierce passion

at whose face we scarce not look
for fear our bones will melt
and hearts explode

and wild joy become our home